"Above the miasmata of a military milieu, Mandy Moe Pwint Tu is a sybil possessed with grief. Homesick for a sick home, she invokes the lore of the land. She laces into her incompetent hosts and omnipresent ghosts. In a blazing display of ပါရမီ [bravura and bravado], she gently coaches us through a transgenerational trauma. Each of her utterances a lesson—in runic risk. Not every first monsoon promises မြေသင်းနံ့ [petrichor]. *Fablemaker* absolutely does."

—ko ko thett, author,
Bamboophobia and *The Burden of Being Burmese*

"Mandy Moe Pwint Tu's striking new poetry collection, *Fablemaker*, is a personal poetic document of the complexities of resistance and cultural identities, memory, and mythologies. As a poet and as a daughter of Burmese parents, the author uses the fable as a vehicle for understanding both trauma and healing. Her skillful use of a variety of forms including the yuzana, a Burmese poetic form, and richly visual language resonates with energy and meaning. *Fablemaker* is an urgent, arresting collection that deftly captures and transforms the challenge of reclaiming one's narrative through an author's unerring eye."

—Maw Shein Win, author, *Percussing the Thinking Jar*

"In her debut poetry collection, *Fablemaker*, Mandy Tu constructs a world where girls speak stars and a father's sadness grows into an ogre. To live in this frozen forest is to befriend trees, to beg the sounds ribbiting out of the water. While a fable centers on its moral, this collection grounds itself in hunger: 'What a thing to tell the hungry, that turns are to be waited for.' The university recruiter has pebbles for eyes. The speaker pays bags of gold to show the west that her country is burning. I have never read a collection that so seamlessly weaves anti-colonial knowledge with the lyric and fantasy. *Fablemaker* is an absolute triumph of a debut, a formally imaginative work with a winding, bright voice."

—Taneum Bambrick, poet, *Intimacies, Received*

"Tu's *Fablemaker* is an instant classic for those familiar with the impossible question of home and the turbulent expanse between the self and what cannot be returned to. These are poems born in that space—somewhere between the vigorously fantastic and the most honest, tender intimacies. There's much to praise and learn from here: surprising image, startling linework, every ending a mic-drop—all working toward a clearer picture of belonging, when 'all you know is how to leave.' There's no one else doing it like Mandy Moe Pwint Tu."

—Steven Espada Dawson, author, *Late to the Search Party*

"Mandy Moe Pwint Tu is a poet of precise image and language. These poems move with surprising grace through different geographies and human identities— daughter to a father, citizen in a time of political instability. The close look at the evolution of relationships with countries of birth and residence, parents, and loss establishes Mandy as a voice well versed in the human and material cost of navigating the complexities of these relationships. A much-needed voice in the world today."

—Ajibola Tolase, author, *2000 Blacks*

"Mandy Moe Pwint Tu's *Fablemaker* is a book that teems with the fantastic—ogres, nagas, garudas, princesses, sentient shadows, and sun-eating dogs—yet somehow it's also a fearless, poignant, and utterly *real* exploration of personal and political struggle. By mixing documentary and lyric-narrative modes, Tu weaves the fabular with the factual to elucidate Myanmar's military coup and the repression that has followed, the life and death of her troubled father, and her own life as a Burmese immigrant in an increasingly xenophobic country. Through brilliant imagination and impeccable craft, *Fablemaker* presents to us a tapestry of the mythical and material monsters that surround and sometimes inhabit us but that we often fail to acknowledge or perceive."

—Sean Bishop, author, *The Night We're Not Sleeping In*

"This is a collection that ticks every box for me, that fires on all cylinders. It's got a voice that's intimate yet eloquent; a style that's daring, embarking on playful experiments with form, but also musical and sensitive to rhythms, both fine and vast, returning again and again to the same obstinate motifs. It speaks from a familiar perspective—that of a foreign student, a daughter bearing the weight of her familial traumas—while at the same time illuminating the epic and turbulent history of Myanmar and our common postcolonial legacy. And though it's filled with the grief of our ruinous times, it still affirms the necessity of fablemaking, of artistic creation that we share as writers."

—Ng Yi-Sheng, author, *Lion City* and *last boy*,
winner of the Singapore Literature Prize

FABLEMAKER

Poems

MANDY MOE PWINT TU

Published by Gaudy Boy LLC,
an imprint of Singapore Unbound
www.singaporeunbound.org/gaudyboy
New York

For more information on ordering books, contact jkoh@singaporeunbound.org.

ISBN 978-1-958652-18-3
eISBN 978-1-958652-19-0

Library of Congress Control Number: 2025937146

Cover design by Flora Chan
Interior design by Jennifer Houle

for my family
|||

CONTENTS

III.

I became a poet to understand how

so close to one another memory and fable can live inside us.

—Maryhilda Obasiota Ibe

DEAR FELLOW FABLEMAKER,

Brush your feet against the moss.

If you sit beneath the ngu-wa tree, you will dream:

golden stupas in an ashen land.

You will wake to rain. Hard on your eyelashes.

Pinging off tin roofs, bent like waves.

There is a father looking for you.

There is a daughter leaving.

If you find yourself at a yellow door,

knock three times. Only three.

Any more and you will scare the cat:

gray as an elephant, blue as the moon.

A mother will invite you in for tea leaf salad.

When she asks you your name, you must not

give it. Instead, look her in her eyes,

shuddering like pond water. The rain

will clatter through the roof.

Ripple in a rusting bucket. Tell her

you come from far away. You have hair

like her son's, dark and curling. You speak

like her daughter. Halting. Unsteady.

She was always falling down.

A mother will ask your name again. Refuse.

Instead tell her a story. This story.

I.

the teller survives
by his telling;

—Li Young Lee

SELWYN

Every time I crack an egg I think of skulls.

How brittle even my father's must have been

under a stronger hand. I think of his hair,

tufted black. Strings of impurities, like white

thread pulling from his earlobes—how they curled

into my palm. Once, we visited a monk,

dawn still clinging to strands of cassia,

who blessed the waters in a silver bowl,

who handed me a leafy branch, saying

let her do it—she is young and pure,

and I tapped the purpling growths

on my father's shoulders, little bumps

the brightest shade of violets. Morning

glories if they burned. I didn't understand

the work of the chanting, but my father's skin

cleared a few soft days later. I want to remember

myself as a loving daughter. Flashbulb grinning

with all my teeth, and him behind the camera.

Dancing on his feet during the ballroom scene

in *Cinderella*. But in every life, a triumph.

A disaster. One night, I breathed in his warmth,

the heat of his tears sticking on the rings

of my neck—realized too late my father

crying. And the house with its yellow

lights, a beckoning. How shame clutches

the lungs and spills against the spine.

How, in every embrace, I seek an exit

marked in amber-gold. This life I have spent

running from my father. I don't ask how much

I've ruined with this looking back.

FABLEMAKING

In the midnights that we miss our mother,
we unfold her memory, lotus-like, in our palms.
In the days before the divorce—or, well, the separation,
she stepped one foot in front of ours, saying *you*
will not slip here, but we fell through the water
hyacinths anyway, stumbled through duckweed,
each grass patch stranger than the last. All ground
is giving when you're running with shadows.
In those days, we trialled many names for our father,
errored each and each: beast, monster, ogre.
But mostly we called him *Dad* because the thing
that possessed him was only a sadder self.
Even then, we knew. This was no work of demons
or evil spirits, although our mother said there had
to be some trifling, some supernatural tinkering,
because why else would a man with string-scarred
fingertips and pondwater eyes abandon a life
he said he wanted? We were young. We leapfrogged
on lily pads, scattered rice grains in the shapes
of birds, only to watch the sparrows spare them.
No matter how hungry, you don't eat your own.
Dad was practically out of the picture, then; a shadow
at the edges. We didn't wait for him to come back.
Those watercress days, we were as safe as tadpoles
bursting from the gossamer, floundering in our changing
bodies, fumbling with the webs on our hands,
drowning on land and in water, long before our gills
came in. Before we learned the cost of breath.

BURMESE PYGMALION

In a dream I'm Eliza Doolittle, selling flowers by Tottenham
Court Road. Here, Henry Higgins wears a familiar face,
shifting in the straggling air. In a breath he's my father, in another

my Uncle Lyndon, my grandfather with the rosehip freckles.
Each hour lolls like marbles in my mouth: glass for the sharpening.
With blackest moss, the flowerpots were thickly crusted, one and all—

say it once, say it perfectly. Waking, scrawl out every grammatical rule
on thinning paper, round letters curving to almost cursive, *i before e
except after c; a sentence must contain a subject and a predicate;*

a sentencing is predicated on the subjected, and if *I* is subject, then—
Dad says *practice makes perfect*, but practice only pins mistakes
into muscle memory. I train my wrist to sweep and curl.

I speak my Burmese in whispers. Learn the verb *decide*
from a grammar book, fold it out on my tongue. In a dream
I'm Eliza Doolittle, coughing out *The rain in Spain stays mainly*

in the plain. Higgins' face changes throughout the years: to teachers
who demand parroted vocabulary, university recruiters with eyes
like pebbles, who say *English literature is difficult for Burmese students*

and mean *it's not for you.* I mispronounce my Burmese, stumble
over our alms-bowl letters, watch my family lift their heads and laugh.
I want to laugh but there are marbles in my mouth. It doesn't matter.

It doesn't matter. Dad will be an ambassador someday. There'll be a ball.
I'll wear a dress that sparkles. With any luck, I'll dance with
a prince. Some linguist will proclaim me royalty

because of my impeccable English. Except of course
he won't. Except he'll say, *Where are you from?* and *Where did you
learn to speak English so well?* and *Can I see your invitation?*

YUZANA FOR THE UNLOVELY

The unlovely, the living
unforgiving. Wounds that close
are those that matter.

Wisdoms scatter in the air
riddling bare. Tell my father—
or rather, show him this.

Human flight risk—a sparrow
sprung with snow. Dead of winter,
polished splinters slipping.

Salt equipping fruitless sky.
The endless *I*, wearing thin.
Let them in who empty

words in the sea. Hands, flatter—
save the tatters. What we owe,
I suppose, forgiving.

THOUGHTS ON REINCARNATION

I want to believe I'm on my last life.
What is nirvana if not a kind of death?

In a past life, a stranger asked the Buddha
for his children. The Buddha offered him his eyes.

Then, pulling the children, screaming,
from the shivering rice barrels, he gave them

away. Did the children ever forgive him?
Did they have to, because he was the Buddha?

I stay awake, listening to my brother's breath
as he sleeps in my corridor. A six-a.m. flight,

a half-hug in the parking lot. I want one more life.
This is the problem with reincarnation:

you don't know if what you've lost
is lost forever. Unless, I guess, you're the Buddha.

His children escaped, by the way. Hid from
their possessor in the cane grass, the silk reeds,

and wove their way back home. I think
they hugged their mother. I think the Buddha

demanded understanding. *I had to,* he likely said.
I wonder who the siblings became in their next life.

I wonder if they stayed together, across this ever-
shortening thread, learning too young that fathers

aren't to be trusted. In each life, the same
karmic cycle. Silk reeds become salt waves become

veranda floors. Their faces, like mine,
like my brother's, hiding from their father,

their bodies pressed against tile and midnight.
One day, they left him, a lonely figure dwindling

in the distance. *I'll see you next life*, a whispered
malediction. It wasn't meant that way. At ten

years old, my brother sits on a rice bag, waiting
for my footsteps. Our father drunk in the next

room. Let it follow that I will not bear these lives
alone. If the Buddha is not the forgiving kind,

then I don't care to be forgiven.

FABLE WITH OGRES

Ogres don't ask for much, only daughters—to sail down lengths

of rivers, to clutch coconuts, buoys in the rising flood. & when

you wash ashore, midnight hair slapped against pallid skin,

fingers bluing at bamboo doors, ogres only ask that you

don't scream. They can't help their fangs, their bleeding gums,

their shadowed eyes, their cheeks, pulsing green. Ogres only want

assistance: someone else's daughter to sweep their floors,

to cook their meals, to pull dandelion fluff from their tangled locks.

Only ask to see the fruits of your labor, each fluttering feather-like

pappus shining in the palm of your hand. Ogres appreciate a hard

worker. Ogres only want to trust you. When they tell you to keep

their attic locked while they're away, they don't actually mind

if you look. Don't care if you turn the bronze key into the wilting

lock, or creak open the ancient door; they'll even let you gasp

at the bones, the skulls, the rotting ligaments on the betel nut floor.

Ogres only want to teach you composure.

RAINDROPS

A window // falling into // bodies, bent &

brittle // limbs like twigs //

storm dust // soot & spittle // elbows striking floors

// house = den // shattered glass = creaking stair //

how much more? // a locked door // poems in pseudonyms

// a raindrop named me // metal, metal // knife

// drunk fist // tug of hair // locked door //

white knuckle walls // burnt wicker // belt buckle

// stumbling, stumbling // locked door // rough,

grumbling // don't leave me // please //

// peeling paint // wire-throttled // whiskey

bottles // some days, the floors swear fealty // others

// broken truces // locked door // purpling

bruises // please // believe me // white

// flags // stoppered pain // an inheritance of hurt //

a stymied grief // a daughter // yearning

// crisscross knees // split // frozen

// a small rhinoceros // upturned bed // frame it //

find him // leave him // father's hand // across my

cheek // i'll redo // the buttons // a brick against

a yellow door // cold cup of coffee // thamee, why don't you call? //

i'm so proud of you // thamee, i'm invincible // i love you

MONSOON DAUGHTER TRIES NARRATIVE THERAPY

On a veranda in Yangon, my mother watches for pigeons.
She hates when they hack at the strings of seeds, mutters:

Greedy bastards. Even the crows are respectful.
They wait their turn.

This, in the heat rising from the pavement,
in the putrid pallor of the monsoon.

What a thing to tell the hungry,
that turns are to be waited for.

My mother bears no love for pigeons,
or men in green coats with eyes like bullets.

Dr. Bardi knows eyes like bullets.
On a mountain in Tennessee, it's hard to see
beyond sandstone as thick as glass.

Dr. Bardi waits six months for a phone call that tells him
he's getting out. Enough of leaves, here. Enough for leaving.

You're going to go, I tell him. He shakes his head.

If I were a ginkgo leaf, I would. You were a ginkgo leaf.

There's belief, and there's promise.
I don't know enough about the two, but he does.

○

At seventeen, I wait for the promise of saltwater,
and a curly-haired boy on a parchment island
declaring sonnets are for eating.

He is skin, and spectacles, and scars,
the silver of a dishwasher in the yellow of a kitchen.

Hand me a ball of string, he says, and changes colour.
Sometimes hatred is a kind of hunger.

○

My brother tastes salt, cayenne, cumin.
Smatters the dust onto his palm, sifts it into boiling.
Peppers each strand of ramen noodle, says

the worst retribution is loss of taste.
I argue he lost his years ago,

quick witted, narrow-eyed, staring through the veil
of spice and steam—

we forget to hold
a funeral for our father.

○

Dr. Bardi says: *call me Al.*
Like I haven't been calling him Al
everywhere except to his face.

But the syllable, the familial
lump in my throat, catches.

I think of things he cannot know.
Think of each feathering prayer

granted, this familiarity; granted,
this wishful, fistful wanting,
granted, a second chance at a father.

Granted, he could leave.
Granted, he could stay.

My aunt is pink shirts and wrinkled skin.
Barrel-boned glasses, eyes like pond water.
She sits beside me when she cries.

We're together on a straw mattress,
my mother screeching thunder.
Something's wrong again.

I'm leaving tonight, my aunt says,
who has nowhere to go.
I'm never coming back.

Sure enough, she packs a bag.
Knocks at the door.

Purgatory—is it this?

◊

My father, in an old tea shop. The monsoons
pelting on the gravel, puddling muddy water.
I nudge my brother, say, *That looks like a crocodile.*

He asks, *Do you think it will eat us?*

My father, empty pockets.
We turn out his wallet,
count each kyat. Childish wailing: *There's enough.*

We rush home, up to our knees
in rainwater. I'm remembering,

I'm remembering.

◊

Once: a princess.

Her lover was eaten by a crocodile.

◊

This was the cost:
a fidgeting daughter in a therapist's office.
Saying, *My father drank. My father hit me.*
Asked, *And now? How are you surviving?*

There are words I must change
my mouth to say.

Is one of them "no"?

Yes.

Older, I am late, opening the door
for my mother on her return from work.
She asks, *What took you so long?*

and I, glib, say, *We didn't care.*
That night, thunder. Crackling
like radio static in our tiny living room.
Mother screaming, *After everything*
I've done for you.

Anger is a tunnel, an echo strapped
to a throat. We called her angry
who only wanted to talk.

Named her after storms who only
needed us to listen.

Say *hurt* in my mother's voice,
and it's a screech. I teach her *trauma*,
trace the letters on her palm.

No, she says. *That's just life.*

I tell Al my favorite Disney movie is *The Little Mermaid*.

Of course it is, he says.

What do you mean?

*Isn't it obvious? The central tension in that movie
is between father and daughter.*

Fourteen years old, I tell my father, *no*,
for the first time.

He's planning a trip to Bangkok, wants me
to come. He's convinced I'm coming, his golden
daughter who loves him despite, despite—

I'll book the tickets. You'll have a great time.

No, I say. It's all I say.

Over the phone, silence like steel.
A thread severs. Flutters flimsy
in the darkness.

Once: a princess.
Cemetery-born, bad omen.
A child with luckless hair.

Her father wanted to protect her.
Built her a tower. Said,
you will be safe here,

didn't count on a prince,
a crocodile, a river.

Didn't count on his daughter
hurling herself off the tower
because her lover died.

Didn't count on their twin fires
and intermingling smoke.

The townspeople said they saw
a rainbow. Her father
knew better.

1988, and the years are rats
running out the clock. A maze
of banners and peacocks,

the same grim men wearing
muted green, holding the same
loaded rifles, staring down

the same, revolutionary eyes.
They were both there,

my mom, my dad.
Calling for democracy.

This is the only story in which
I imagine them together,
and believe it.

Belief is a psychiatrist.
Belief says, *I know humour*

is one of your coping mechanisms,
but it would really help us now

if you wouldn't joke.

I'm remembering:

Dad used to say, *A promise is a promise.*
Commercial airline, sepia undertones,
a figure of a man running home
to his four-year-old daughter.

Of course, he never kept them.

                                               ◍

At twenty, I love a man with the name
of a fictional character. He liked film:
viewed the world through a Dutch angle.

Slightly lopsided, like his kisses.
Picture-perfect, striped T-shirt,
here was love like a jacaranda tree,

pooling purple, bristling abundance.
I put an ocean between us. Something
about drowning and sunken ships.
I played that metaphor to death.

No one tells you how freeing it is
to stop loving someone.

                                               ◍

I post a poem to Facebook, about
Mother's Day—a song of survival.
Raised voices and clenched fists,

bone crashing skin. Running
when home is the mouth
of a crocodile. Leave your shoes.

Cross the river. Pray we make it
to the other side.

A stranger tells me, *Thank you.*
I ran away from my husband
in the middle of the night with nothing
but my passport because that was the night
he was going to kill me.

Cut to my mother, on the other end
of a computer screen:

How dare you. Take that poem down.
What if your father reads it?
You'll kill him.

I almost say, *Good.*

This isn't the first time
you've died. One summer, hunched
over a sink, mother told me
you had liver cancer, not knowing

earlier that summer I'd written
a play, a five-minute caricature

of our lives, given your character
liver cancer, a few months to live.

Finally, a time for re— re—
union? signation? cognition?
I have to Google *reconciliation*

but all I wanted to imagine then
was you, dying. Was you, dead.

All I wanted to do was mourn you
even though you were still living.

What was that you said, Dad,
about love?

Meet me in the middle.

Once, a monsoon daughter.
A whiskey-drenched crown her father
brought her from Singapore
settling heavy on her head.
When he dies, she will remember this.

Play it back.
Play it all back.

DIAGNOSIS

Grayscale memory
Dad's callouses
facing the doctor
Show him
circus animal
a girl glitters
marches across
I spend hours
same shiny
Show him
open your palms
flat like lily pads
mine like
aslant, askew
means you can
never receive.
white, the doctor
radioulnar
Dad asking *how*
do we fix her
banyan roots
the forcing apart
in surgery, she
the bones will
refuse to stay
or albatrosses;
of piano teachers
to compensate
keep them down

tile, cement
clutching forearms
without a face
put out your hand
party trick
in sequins
a tightrope
emulating her,
dress, falling.
your hands,
Dad's hands
on pond water
banana fronds
bent at an angle
never ask fully,
X-rays, black &
saying *congenital*
synostosis
do we fix it
bones like intertwined
chopsticks before
No point
will only feel pain
stick again, re-fuse
apart, like magnets
the continued chagrin
when elbows rise
for restricted movement
your fingers must

25

hover over the keys
so I try
the bones, say
a fusion
does it matter
sounds the same?
All the great kings
You are destined
but I knew
all it could ever mean
sticking, something
stuck, twisting
than you were

like so, like so, like—
to explain without naming
stuck together
(confusion)
when the music
Dad at my side,
had this affliction.
for greatness,
all it meant
was something about
about staying
to go a little further
meant to go.

INTERNATIONAL STUDENT

To feast on visas means you are never full

The United States Embassy stands guarded by barbed wires and metal detectors

I carry a sign to a #StopAAPIHate protest that reads

I DID NOT PAY $360 IN VISA FEES TO GET FUCKING HATE CRIMED

A white man with a camera takes a video, calls it *pithy*

Microsoft Word keeps autocorrecting to *pity*

Citrus fruits are often pithy

My mother brings me oranges in a life I lived too long ago

To take the TOEFL, I sit in a dark room with six other hopefuls speaking the colonizer language into our headsets

No one warns the boy beside me that the first time the lady's voice comes on, it's just for voice recognition so he keeps telling her his name

The U.S. wants to know if I can speak English, so it charges me $325 to prove it

I pay $325 to say I understand words like *pithy*

I carry my passport and copies of my visa in a folder in my backpack

I pay $1,500 in flight expenses to get called *chink* before a conference presentation

On a panel we are asked if we have ever faced a microaggression

My mother packs me rabbit wool sweaters because it'll be colder where I am

I pay $1,600 in scholarship taxes each year to say *I belong* through my teeth

USCIS would rather I earn no royalties while on my F1 visa

In the land of the free, your trauma is worth nothing

Some days I get mad that my alma mater won't hire an international international student advisor

At night for fear of deportation I pray to a god in another country who couldn't get a visa here

I pay $10 in official academic transcripts so I can call universities my "alma mater"

My body shuts down trying to process, charges me $30 in French fries

I still pay $1,600 in segregated fees to write poems about how my country is burning

I keep joking I'm going to accidentally get a doctorate

My mother keeps my diplomas up on a glass shelf, asks for more photographs so she can brag

In her dreams I'm a professor on that mountain in Tennessee

A U.S. immigration lawyer tells me to wrench the F1 for all it's worth

She says *if you're going to do a PhD, you might as well do it before you start working*

As a Humanities scholar I get to pay $470 for one year of work authorization to keep writing poems about how my country is burning

STEM scholars get three years and they don't even write poems

My mother's doctors tell her she's depressed but she refuses to go to a psychiatrist for fear of more medication

To make my mother happy I decide I'm going to be an academic

I pay $260 in state taxes so I can teach poems about how the West has forgotten my country

An admissions officer asks, *What advice do you have for an incoming international student to the U.S.?*

When they call you alien, they fucking mean it, no matter how many poems you drop at their feet

ON BEING ABSENT FOR THE REVOLUTION

Spring Revolution back home
—and I am here. Wrapped up and wilting
in fading daffodils, twilight-tripping and trillium-tied.
Back home, the *padauk* is blooming, her golden tresses
the kind of wealth that hope affords. Even this tree
is useful.

      —But I am here,
nestled nicely in narcissus, rippled with redbuds,
shaking cherry blossoms from their boughs. Back home,
blood is water spilled from flesh. Flowers bloom
in the wake of the dead, but will they wake?
But I wake

      —I wake here.
Spring outside my window, winter boughs sprouting green.
These balding cypress knees are nothing compared
to the knees of my people, their bodies thudding
with the glint and sear of metal through their heads.
Hail the victorious dead and sand the roads.
Let the blood lead a little ways, then nowhere.
See, these roads can lead

      —oh, nowhere.
The way home is closed. But spring is here,
on this unsalted earth. On this daisy dotted grass,
where dandelions still hold wishes for puckered lips.
No gunshots in the night here, no shards of glass
on my bedroom floor. No thunder of pots and pans
in the dead of night. My skin is clean, unstitched.
My conscience tainted, not my body. My scars
my own. No scars for home. My mother knows

where I am.

I am not with her.

DEAR FELLOW FABLEMAKER,

Death pecks at every door.

I imagine him young: a cuckoo bird

raised in a mortal nest. Gray feathers,

bright beak. He came for my father,

asleep in a bed as blue as oxygen

tanks. Pressed his ear against his chest.

Said, *It's time.* My father refused. Said,

My children aren't home. I have

to stay. The only time he'd wanted to.

The only time he couldn't. Death

pulled out his spirit from his throat.

His glasses settling still against

his nose. The tiles beneath him

still amber. Through the window,

the clattering of a train against

a railway track. A symphony.

Death asked, *Any final requests?*

My father's hands, limp at his sides.

I want to be remembered.

Silence, and a whirring fan.

II.

And the wars will stop. And everyone
will do the dishes.

—Sean Bishop

MY FATHER DIED

surrounded by
nobody. Perhaps an echo or two
of a girl, a boy. Hums of guitar strings

> thrumming the air. The oxygen
> didn't enter his veins
> fast enough.

> Not the oxygen's fault.

My father used to smoke cigarettes,
military green. The brand: *Apple*.
As in, *the apple doesn't fall far*

> no matter how hard it tries.

I don't like the way my father died.
Loveless, alone. The world he knew
crumbling into smoke, နိုင်အရေး နိုင်အရေး

> but only for the living.
> Survived by his living
> daughter, loving son.

I know. I write too often
about the dead.

CONFESSIONS

This life I spend trying not to hurt my mother.

I dry my hair before bed.

Track my menstrual cycle.

Take her side in Facebook arguments.

Pretend I didn't hate my father.

When she says *you're lucky* and *don't come back* in the same breath,

I take it as permission to be selfish.

I live alone so I have room to cry.

On the phone with her my brother lies about

how much the taxi to my apartment cost. He tells her, *Twenty dollars*

but holds up three fingers to me. Each concession, translated.

It's how we know we're related. I tell him but not her

when I go to protests. Forget to mention my ankle sprain.

She asks *do you have enough money* and I never say no.

Instead I write long posts on Facebook for her birthday.

Reuse the same five pictures. Try to forget I haven't seen her

in seven years. This is the law of protection, enacted across oceans:

My mother asks to read my poems. I forget to send them.

DEAR FELLOW FABLEMAKER,

This is how I receive the news:

on a bed in Memphis, Tennessee,

red curtains blocking out the sun.

My brother's message on my phone:

Did you hear? Are you all right?

Then, slowly, the story: my father was sick.

He was sick, and everyone was sick.

In a country choking for air,

his wife brought it home with her.

But she was young. He was older.

They met in my childhood, when

the light was harsh but the rain

was soft. He took her to a movie.

He brought her home with him.

Then he was sick, and there was only

an oxygen tank. Blue as the eye

of a peacock feather. Hope as sure

as a yellow door. He woke,

and he was well. Said, *Cancer couldn't*

kill me, and neither will this.

Then Death knocked. Sung him

away. They took his body to the outskirts

of the city, where body upon body

burned together. Who marks

where he passed? I wasn't going

to tell this story. I laughed when he died—

relief a mangled gurgling.

WHEN I AM A MOTHER

When I am a mother,
I will tie my daughter's hands together
and press them to her lips.
She will learn to sing through her teeth
and beg a world forgotten.

I will tell her that down by the old banyan tree
her father swallowed three stray bullets
and made them part of him.
Tell her that mettle isn't always what it looks like
or what it's supposed to be.

When she tells me she will change the world,
I will take her to the muddy ripples
of the Ayeyarwady and teach her
the meaning of a single droplet.

These girls are too used to monsoons,
to being too much too often.
What happens when the drought
settles on their skin,
when rainwater tastes like vinegar
and dust is breath to choke on?

When I have a daughter
I will baptize her in this country's blood,
drench her from head to toe
so she never dreams of escape.
When the earth is in her bones

and these sorrows in her gums
I will give her betel nut to chew.

She will count each feathered crow
that soars over the Shwedagon
and find no poetry. Find no song.
She will look and know.

DEAR FELLOW FABLEMAKER,

My country is governed by a constitution,

marked by green hands in the year 2008.

Provisions on a state of emergency—imagine then,

a wet market, whiskered catfish still shuddering

in shallow water, metal buckets holding three,

five at a time. A young man sells sugarcane juice

in plastic bags, plastic straws dipped for the slurping.

In my country, it's so hot we send a celestial dog

to consume the sun. My mother braids her hair

during eclipses. Here, *the president may, if necessary,*

declare a military administrative order, their coats

the greens of pea shoots. We fry them up, lured

onto our plates with sesame oil. In a blackout,

we slumber hungry. Radio static lullabies, snippets

of hushed voices. In my country, the sky is brighter

than the earth. *The National Defense and Security*

Council shall exercise the sovereign power in the name

of the President. In our defense, we forgot our names.

Security is a locked door, a bolted gate, and a guard

dog waiting. Sovereign a plastic tiara that will not fit

my head. Once I fell in love and my grandfather wrapped

a rosary around my wrist. Whichever spirit possessed me

possessed me no longer. Love: *restrict or suspend as required.*

A face I called mother. A father I called dead. Suspend this:

body enclosed within an hour of his death. *Restrict or suspend,*

as required, one or more fundamental rights of the citizens.

A train ride to Naypyitaw, months after the city's renaming.

The emptiest capital. We stood on the road and watched

the fog descend, blue on the plains. My father's glasses,

fogged up whiskey bottles. *Restrict, suspend*: breath.

How wrought, how stoppered. This was a state of emergency,

and these were the provisions. Dear fellow fablemaker,

the legitimate measures of . . . any military body . . . on behalf

of the Commander-in-Chief of the Defense Services . . .

while a declaration of emergency is in operation

shall be valid. No legal action shall be taken on such

legitimate measures. In my country, girls with stars for names

die like the rest of us. Bullets break like water.

YUZANA FOR THE DEFEATED

Surrender takes shadowed shapes:
grasping raw grapes with your hands,
storms like sands, winged and armed.

Ask the harm of summer songs.
Throats belong in beechen green,
wars between the waters.

Say we faltered in the dark.
Stumbles stark with worrying—
You're burying us fast.

The last raindrop like hunting,
confronting, shatters, shrivels.
You bathe each bristled bone.

Call the hurt your own. The swarm,
the sweep. Alarmed pots and pans
bark commands. Who escapes?

IT'S A BAD YEAR FOR THE GINKGOES

But they live to try again.
Each near-yellow leaf
settles on the ground
with its kindred. Green heart,
gold brow. What can we ask
of them that we can't ask
of ourselves? In Myanmar,
an elderly man curls fetal—
dead by any estimation, in a blue
United Nations shirt. In a play,
the devil wears a leopard print.
I always want to fuck the men onstage,
but they're never single. They hold
my hands while they mouth,
Thank you. I save my goodbyes
until the last, last minute. In this life,
my father waits by a different door
for my arrival. *Come play the piano,*
he says. *I want to hear you play.*
I never pick up when he calls.
In an elevator, Elijah Bean pulls out
the yellow aventurine I got him.
He doesn't like its jagged edges
splintering his pockets, but he carries it.
It must help, he tells me. Two nights ago,
I downloaded ancient voicemails
just to hear my father breathe. Half
a chuckle, in the midst of honking cars
and rustling linen shirts. Facebook

Messenger lists all the calls I ignored.
Suggests: *Missed call. Call back?*
Missed call. Call back? Missed call.
Call back? It's true. I hurt my father.
In the winter I watch the ginkgoes
bare their arms to the snow. Press
my palm to their bark. Beg mercy,
mercy, mercy.

KIN MA

In June 2021, BBC News reported that 200 of the 240 homes in Kin Ma Village in central Myanmar were razed to the ground by the Burmese military.

Where to begin? Who was cruel, who was crueler?
Who was awake when they lit the torches?

      We left our grandmothers with the torches.
      We showed them how to keep the light.

We left them in the house. We left by moonlight—
We left them food and drink for a day or two.

      They did not survive a day or two.
      The soldiers came with rage and fire.

The floors went up in smoke. Their skin on fire—
Maybe they died in their sleep. Maybe they prayed.

      Oh, God, there is no question. Of course they prayed.
      —Ashes to ashes and dust to dust—

Not enough. We've had enough of ash and dust.
Let's begin. If they are cruel, then we'll be crueler.

FABLEMAKING

Before we learned the cost of breath,
we gulped down pond water. Stuck our tongues out,
caught fireflies by the throat, glowing down
our gullets. The only way to keep the light
is to steal it yourselves. Now and then we stuffed them,
wings and abdomen and all, into a jar, to keep by our mother's bed.
But even we couldn't command the imprisoned, more
beetle than butterfly, to glow at will—and so they languished,
and Mother threw their thoraxes to the wild grass
for the birds to eat. Even here, a cycle. When we sprouted
antennae, our flesh hardening into callous amber,
Mother tugged at her hair and swept us into a mason jar.
You'll be safe here, she promised, but we tapped at the glass,
our reflections renumbering, the deepening in our eyes
creating distortions, until we no longer remembered
what we looked like before, so we clung to each other,
clutching our wings, asking *what if we tore them off?*
Then our father came, a thundering in our brittleness,
and Mother shoved us under the bed—clattering,
quiet, breath breaking in shattered spurts. His voice,
a crackling: *Where are they?* And we imagined him
spider, lizard, frog, but he was a garuda bird—bigger
than houses, his feathered wings scooped us out
from the darkness, and we screamed, his beak unfurling,
lily-like, and he emptied us into his mouth. And weeping,
we bled, and bled, and bled, coating the buds on his tongue,
so he wrung us in spit and hissed us out. This was the day
we learned that monsters can be hurt. When he left,
Mother sat with us in the darkness, patching up

our unbroken skin, still glimmering golden, saying,

Once upon—and we told our stories in the candlelight.

FABLE WITH FROGS

On February 10, 2024, Myanmar's military junta announced it would mandate conscription for the first time since the People's Military Service Law was passed in 2010. Under the law, all men aged 18–35 and women aged 18–27 are eligible to serve in the armed forces for at least two years.

—The Diplomat

Begin: a family of frogs, sitting nervously

together. Once, the pond was a puddle,

but the gravel gave way beneath plodding

wheels, and the rains that came did not know

how to cease. Enter: snakes with rifles,

green as jackfruit skin. Saying, *Give us*

your son. Hunger grips us like water.

Mother Frog weeping, clutching her son's

webbed feet, her tongue like bamboo shoots

in her mouth. *He's too young,* she begs.

Please. He's my only son. Who will rub balm

on my joints on rainy days? Who will sit with me

when the thunder clamours so loud it shakes

the ground? Who will protect me when

the burglars clamber over our netted wall to steal

the last of my mother's jewels? But the snakes

unhinge their jaws. They swallow him whole.

SAVAGE

Savage, my father
moves a raindrop off-kilter.
By raindrop I mean a universe—
his & mine, both, pillared by something
other than blood. Or only blood.
But sixteen years later, the weight
of wafting air against my cheek.
An almost shifted jawline. Buttons
on a stranger's floor. In my mind I was no older
than three, but I was ten. See how the brain
rewrites itself. See how I'm self-correcting.
Today I'm obsessed with prolepsis,
from all the years I watched each raindrop
curl back skyward only to splatter against
our thin, tin roof. All the days crushing pink
pills into whiskey glasses. Petrichor, alcohol—
the words sitting so closely on my tongue,
I often mistake one for the other.

OUT WITH LANTERNS

1.

These days every sparrow
is a bird from my past.
Once, I pulled one,
flurried & feathered,
from the water.
Left a prayer:

Let me be saved
like once I saved you.

2.

At the museum, three Buddha statues.
Golden script scrawling on their daises,
a clattering of offering bowls & upturned
mouths. I press my palms together
to these lacquered figures & pray.
Words settle on the glass between us,
but I'm not sure they hear.

3.

On Thadingyut I call my brother
to say, *I think I'm homesick.*
He returns, *Me too.*

4.

The tender art of candle-tilting
I learned very young.

Hold by the stem, wait
for the wax to melt. Watch
for footprints, candlelit
& celestial, on makeshift stairs.

Step by step, the Buddha
weaves home to his mother.

5.

The USCIS agent
calls across the room:
*I can't find
her country.*

Slowly he moves
my fingers, pressed & rolling,
across a scanner. Huffs, frowns.
Much of the imprint
is white space, so we try again.

I explain the absence—
throttled between my ribs,
a yearning I'm still trying
to voice. One more time.
One more time. One more:

I want to say *I'm sorry,
I'm so sorry. I'm just not
fully here.*

PAGODA

A
divine

can be
a country.

But mine? Each
rain-tipped finial

an invitation for lightning-
wielding demons. I invoke

ogres in my midnight prayers
peittas who jostle rice grains

at needlepoint. They beg my country
for a single string of coconuts

I leave at the shrine: *be full.*
Eyes in the edges—*aren't you staying?*

I press gold leaves on already gilded stupas.
Pour water on nats at my Thursday corner.

If leaving was a summons, what called me away?
This blessing, this curse: the clamour at my back:

Unravel at the roots, bow your head to white marble.
A divine can be a country which cannot be yours.

BECOMING CALIBAN

Miranda's shallow & Prospero's a jerk.
Ferdinand carries logs & everyone's like *Oh what a gentleman.*
Caliban's the colonized underdog, so I'm supposed to love him.
It's Shakespeare class. Our Prospero instructs, *Create a Caliban*
& disappears in a wisp of smoke. She has a dog: let's call her
Ariel. Ariel has severe separation anxiety. Ariel watches
Stephano & Trinculo decide they're too white for Caliban,
although neither actually says it. I pull on a loose shirt
& they hurl a net over me. I dab a seaweed mask on my face,
already fracturing on my temples. Steph has a melody
pulled up. *We want to make sure he doesn't come off as entirely
human*, he says. Trinculo's the one who brought the net.
Borrowed it from the theatre department's costume shop.
You ready? asks Prospero & I shuffle into the classroom,
its off-white walls & too-white faces. Cue laughter. Cue
Caliban—in turn upright, then hunching, then crumbling.
A performance, they think. *A performance,* I tell myself.
Stephano & Trinculo & their white teeth. I mention the irony
to Prospero & she exclaims, *I thought of that!* It's not for her
to think about the things I carry: *Hag-seed, hence! A devil,
a born devil, on whose nature / Nurture can never stick!
Fucking chink. Where did you learn to speak English?*
Stephano & Trinculo, too white, used to never asking.
& *Ban, Ban, Ca-Caliban! (How fine my master is!)*
How is it that I can only dream in their tongue?

IN WHICH THE WHITE MAN ON MY THESIS DEFENSE COMMITTEE ASKS ME ABOUT NATION

after Noor Hindi

1. And why does it matter when *nations* don't exist?
   a. The Myanmar passport ranks 98th on the Henley Passport Index.
   b. I spend my life looking for an escape hatch.
   c. Visas cost gallons in saltwater.

2. When you speak of harm, is it a *national harm*?
   a. Who inflicts harm? Who receives it?
   b. My mother sees a soldier in the street and hurries back to the fourth-floor apartment she shares with my aunt.
   c. 19,434 people died of Covid-19 in Myanmar, my father only one of thousands.

3. How does love—or lack of love—for a country translate to fiction or poetry?
   a. My country is a woman, golden-winged and dancing in the night sky.
   b. My country is a seventeen-year-old girl, a bullet in her head, a corpse holding up three fingers. Even in death, a defiance.
   c. My country is a metaphor I thread each violence through.

4. Do you consider yourself Burmese-American?
   a. No.
   b. If the hyphen between the words could halve the burden of a balancing act. If a stretch of ink could denote the kind of wholeness I crave. If I could be both, and. If I could be. And.
   c. In this life, I dream of a homecoming. A plane, taxiing to a stop. Someone speaking to me in Burmese. I don't understand all of it. I don't need to.

5. Tell us about *imagination.*

    a.   An image: a girl loving her country with every corrupted skin cell. Her country loving her back, with every shard of bloodstained pavement.

    b.   I am with my father when he dies. I forgive him. I carry his body to the crematorium on the outskirts of town. Watch him rise as smoke.

    c.   I present to you // the clatter // of a poet // trying to imagine // something other than // suffering

YUZANA FOR THE LEFT BEHIND

Sunflowers last forever.
North, the farmers sow yellow
seeds. In Bago, the sun

rises under threat. Gunshots
ring out, the air hot and veiled—
the summer stale with salt.

The leavers, at fault; at risk
the left-behind sister, she
is lonely, is harried.

They could have carried the girl
across now, the world over,
fed her clover to live.

How do you forgive? The sun
is still bright, still as yellow.
She'll grow. She'll know better.

DEAR FELLOW FABLEMAKER,

This is my darkest memory: my father

bathed in bright fluorescent lights,

on his side, on the carpet. He's drunk

and telling me a story: A tiger marries

a tigress, and this was a bad idea.

The tigress seeks another beloved,

although the tiger has no evidence

that this is true. Only that the tigress

jogs in the park outside their apartment,

only that she sits with her books, working

towards her master's degree. So the tiger,

who already has another beloved,

well before he ever suspected the tigress,

who leaves evidences of infidelity in his pockets

for his wife to find, must decide to leave her.

What did I think, I, who must leave with him?

Fear tastes like orange peel, sharp and bright.

Later, my therapist says: *Children know what*

they're born for. My mother tells me she took

a pill and I unfurled, like rain-riddled

gardenias in her womb—but the cord that should

have tethered us bound me, instead,

to my father. This, she says, is the tragedy.

III.

I'm, you know, still here,
tulip, resin, temporary—

—Jean Valentine

THIRD SPRING

in response to Ilya Kaminsky's "We Lived Happily During the War"

I sit   in summer,
stalled, statuesque.

In a poem   I summon
a pile of bodies

touched with blood,
clumped   and wet—

tall enough   to climb over.

In Bagan,   the pagodas
drown. Each golden temple

an upturned cup
suspended in spillage.

In her apartment my mother
moves   the tables

away from the windows.
A lifetime ago   there were

mangoes   knocking with the rain.
But the cyclone comes,

spins gunfire   streaking
from the sky. Every day

an airstrike—on hands
that might have wrung

poems,   feet that might
have waded   through lake water,

eyes that could have read Kaminsky

and cried, *We lived.*

FABLEMAKING

Once, we told our stories in the candlelight.
We had no choice—electricity, stored enough
in baubles, broke at our touch. And the cry rang out
across the township, over the tinning roofs of the city,
a cry we mistook, even as the bulbs flamed fluorescent,
for *He's coming*. So we hid under the wicker,
tucked our toes under blankets, and waited for the huff
of a father too close to home. All we ever needed: the suggestion
of a flicker, for when our skin moved with the grass,
camouflaging against the slit-yellow eyes of predators.
The less seen, the safer. We wanted to become the wind,
but we grew fangs in all the wrong places, tousled and soft—
wolves with no bite. Each midnight howl a question:
what is wrong with us? and *can anybody hear?* The echoes:
Here, here, here, in his voice, the beckoning of a snarl,
the breadcrumbs disappearing in the dirt. We knew better
than to go chasing. Instead, we peeled stars from the sky,
chewed them up and spat them out. Too sharp for our tongues,
still learning the taste of iron, we who only lived in the cold,
unused even to the heat of the wormholes. So we made
our stories: girls who spoke stars and boys who ate them,
and never mind that it was dark forever. And Mother slept
to the lilt of our voices, strangling on stories that starred her
until they didn't. Later we made lanterns from the scales peeling
off our backs and she tugged them off and we screamed
because it hurt, because it mattered then when the ending began.

AT SIXTY, MY MOTHER

wears her hair down, like the weeping willow
I say I'll be when I'm dead. I tell her I want
waves like hers, and not the stringent strings
currently pulling from my head. She says
it was late—much later in life when the rivers
on her scalp became oceans: all saltwater
and seaweed, constantly crashing, curling,
recurring. At sixty, my mother asks if I'll
keep her age a secret. As if the years are unattended
candle flame. As if they'll blow out any second, or
burn the house down, and there won't be enough
hair on her head to put the fires out. She says oceans
are best watched from a distance, remembers
gripping sand and debris when years ago
she watched the pink, flushed horizon and
floated out with the current, before the waves
took her under. Tried to take her out, but
at sixty, my mother recalls only the taste
of salt. Talks about the sea like she's never
seen it before, says one day my hair will
curl a little, like hers, says one day I, too,
will carry oceans on my head.

YUZANA FOR THE WATCHING

Surveillance is a wonder.
This thundering, crackling light.
Ours a fight for viewing.

Each corpse renewing alone.
Call home in emergencies.
Breath like leaves, descending.

We're defending dying dreams.
Every scream a lullaby
we catch in skies that shift.

Fingers sift through piles of sand.
Yours a hand I cannot hold.
How cold your passing is.

Yet only this skin bluing.
I'm accruing wounds like nights.
Catching flights that sunder.

FABLE FOR A FATHER

One day I grew scales. My father grew feathers.

In our living room, we became what the other

hated. He said, *You're my daughter so I can eat you.*

I said, *I will dive so deep into the ocean you will never*

find me. Impasse, but not really. He bared his wings.

I ran to the water. He was hungry. I was sorry.

When he died, I found a feather tucked under

my scales. I named it grief. I wrote with it.

FABLEMAKING

It mattered then when the ending began:
a story told in reverse decries an unbecoming.
First: the happily ever after, then the monsters,
the shedding scales, the wings, the fur, the tails.
Say defeat isn't always guaranteed, say this
is the only way to live. How easily we could say now,
neither of us believing we were ever children.
Each of us knowing only we had the other.
Us with a mother trembling into fish scales
on the nights the saltwater stained her pillows,
when she left her shining on the stark, straw mats.
A father who clawed at his ribcage to beg his heart
for an understanding. A heart that beat its wanting,
thundered him half to death. At the beginning
of the ending, we clutched kitchen knives and slept
with them in our tiny fists, too wary then of the night,
and its ferrying ogres with fang-tipped teeth. Our mother
gave us lotus buds for the underside of our tongues—
for protection, she said. But our father still hurled
bricks at our doors, despite the holy water, despite
the prayers, but when we touched him we startled
to find his hair, now silvering; his hands, now wrinkled.
And were we monsters then who never inherited
his particular brand of savagery? His memories became
ours, unwillingly, each guitar string sorrow quenched
in the mouth of a willing siren—sweet summer whiskey
drenched in the depths of her hair. And he rasped and rasped,
understand? understand? understand? but we didn't, we couldn't
with our firefly brains and our fishhook hearts, we only wanted

to be a part of this loving—and we clasped our mother's hands,

when rubies tumbled from her lips, and she said *make a wish,*

make a wish, make a wish, we wished and wished and forgot

what we wished for, until the earth grasped our feet

and the ocean spilled hot between us and we lost her

and him and we screamed because this wasn't what we wanted,

but too late, we sit with our fingers dipped into the sun.

Our faces, green with bioluminescent longing.

DEAR FELLOW FABLEMAKER,

My mother was young. She begged

her friend for one of her brothers.

Let me marry one of them, she cried,

in the slant-gray of the cloud light,

in the crimson of the hibiscus,

how it reflects on her cheeks—

Dear fellow fablemaker, there were

three brothers. The eldest, already

married. The third a soldier. The second

brother played the guitar and spoke

English. He wanted a wife. They met

in the ancient house on U Loo Nee Street,

black wooden planks and a piano, ringing

just out of tune. The linoleum yellow

under their feet. He asked her name. She

gave it. In a month, they were married.

Small ceremony, and the walls the wrong

colour. In her wedding photos, she looks

decorated and solemn. Her father refused

to attend, although her mother begged him to.

In my country, women don't challenge

their husbands. My mother will remember

this for the rest of her life, on the days

her new husband tugs at her hair

as she stumbles down a staircase,

as he locks her out amid a snowstorm,

as he raises a chair over his head,

his breath hot and spitting whiskey.

I will remember this for the rest of my life:

my mother on the veranda swing, her hair lit

amid the star jasmines, the lady slipper orchids,

asking, *Are you sure it's okay that I left your father?*

Even as I answer: *Yes. Yes. Yes.*

CREMATING OUR FATHERS

In Burmese, the word for sun
also means stay.

When you imagine death,
you don't imagine this:

body on a platter,
headfirst into the flame,

spirit wailing at the smoke,
mistaking sunbeams for hellfire—

someone calling out your name,
begging နေပါ နေပါ နေပါ॥

But all you know is how to leave.
All you remember is the sun.

ALL THE THINGS YOU'VE MISSED

I am still a daughter.
A woman in a mask
needled ginkgo leaves
into my arm. Your arm.
Your mother's arm.
If this action echoes back
through my ancestry,
ghosts of gold leaves
will flicker on your skin.

I paid $500 for new pairs
of glasses. I told Mom
they cost $100. I've taken
to lying. I learned that
from you. A doctor
tells me to keep an eye
on glaucoma. I almost
laugh. Instead I blame
my near-sight on your genes.
Even now, there are things
I can't see. I stumble
off-balance when I walk.
The chamomile on the pavement
too green. A parent penned
a quote on cement, in pink chalk.
Something about patience.

I think about how you said
you would never die. How

in the breath before your faltering,
you must have thought
you had survived.
I sleep on midnight
blue sheets, the color—I guess—
of your oxygen tank.
What did breath cost, Dad,
in the end?

I still keep watch. I light
a candle every year. Cook
an omelet over the stove, eat
with my hands, slick with canola
oil and salt. Al marvels at my memory.
I can't even remember the year
my parents died, he says.

There's a story which goes: a girl pulled out
of the Seine, beloved for her pallor,
became a death mask. In death,
a kind of peace. They put her face
on CPR dolls. Named her,
so that others pulled from the river
could be loved while they were living.

Dad, did you make me a poet
so you could live? Which of us
is the face pulled from the river?
Which of us the hand that loved it?

DEAR FELLOW FABLEMAKER,

There is a country drowning. Mine.

The rains came with a vengeance,

flame tree blossoms splotching

the earth, washing betel nut spit

off the pavement. Taxi wheels

in the flood, still spinning.

We build our houses on stilts.

Enter the mouths of crocodiles

to see our beloveds. Even as lightning

strikes the telephone poles. Even as we hunger

from inside the belly of the beast. How pink

its flesh. How slant its blood.

How sharp our teeth.

HISTORIES

In 1988 our fledgling nation drowned again in blood and clamshell clanging, oh how holy the flesh on pagoda stairs

I ask for a country, nothing else

On the night my parents met, I dream my mother dancing—water lilies blooming at her feet, my father's lips spilling with rubies

At fourteen I make simplistic art for the love of oppressors

Mud clings to my brother's legs as he runs from a ranine symphony, the croaking frogs drowning out the gunfire

When a thief stole our electrical generator, we forgave him and forgave him—all he'd wanted was light, was light

All we ever cried for was rain

My father is a revolutionary in a life salted with sorrow—a wooden house buckling under the weight of bougainvillea

I demand justice for the living, forgiveness from the dead

My mother hits her head on the doorframe and bleeds—a hand over my mouth, the taste of blood like sugar cane, sticking on my tongue

In 1940 my grandmother married a man who would sell her childhood home

All her life, on the verge of tears, babbling her tale to anyone who would listen, begging *I want to go home I want to go home I want to go home*

I imagine a greater world and sell it to the highest bidder

At six I tell my grandmother *This is your home and there is your husband* but I don't know yet what exile means

In our dreams, my brother and I are back in that yellow-walled house, with its lone parlor pillar, its marble backyard

They say Aung San Suu Kyi played the piano when she was under house arrest, her fingers poised over ivory teeth

In another country, my father doesn't die choking on his own spit

Give us your broken, your limbless, your browning bodies crumbling into ditches; give us your rice paper sisters, your tea leaf brothers, your sesame seed children (one more for the pile)

In February 2021 I stop complaining about my country

When my grandmother dies in a stranger's house, her daughter says *I cried earlier*—I want the women in my family to marry better men

In another country I am a poet who writes only about gardenias

WINTER AGAIN

And it was all right.

And the men I crush on are far too old for me.

And the water that drums against the glass is ochre,

and my father's blood is bubbling inside his body.

And the cat nudges me out of her chair, curls into a crescent moon, and mewls
asleep,

and in the last dream I remember I am running late.

And a body I don't recognize is on the news again, and an eye has fallen out of its
socket,

and a young boy weeps wordlessly on my mobile screen,

and cement is a honey cake I forgot to bake for Christmas. And the bombs
thunder

and the rain huddles under a sky fraught with phosphorus,

and my brother hangs his buckwheat noodles to dry on the rack.

And I am in love again with my hand in the bonfire,

and the man I love is looking over the lake at the drowning stars and whistling a lament his father wrote, one listless autumn day.

And it's New Year's and I wrench my heart from my ribs,

and wringing I toss it across the water.

I WAS ALWAYS A POET WITH A DEAD FATHER

My first love poem was a poem for my father.

He was young like me.

He was young until me.

When he died, he stammered ash.

The kind we begged to keep.

The kind we couldn't.

What use have I for a living father?

Present like the sun, beloved,

watching sparrows bend the grass.

Some other life he sees where I am now.

He's proud. My epigraphs are lines

he approves of. *My poet daughter*, he says.

Just like her father. I break my father's

memory on frozen lakes. Cast it over

the cattails. How thin his hair.

How soft his flesh. In lieu of an epitaph

I want to know what happened to his glasses.

Whether his last words were a poem.

And if I say they were? Across the sea

his ghost waits in a yellow-walled house.

A man, still lonely. Old as a country.

Young as a nation. He takes a breath

I am still holding.

FABLE WITH ORANGES

If you feed a tree a skeleton, in the summer

it bears the sweetest oranges. My grandmother

peels them, tendril by tendril. The juice gleams

down her chin. I am grateful for this memory

that isn't quite a true one. In the mornings,

I watch her braid her hair. The climbing sun

drains the darkness from her tresses. She says, *I don't*

need it anymore, do I? The sky needs much more than any of us

can give. If I strain, I remember her voice. A lilt like that

of black-capped chickadees. In her name, I give—

a river-full, a pebble-slant. The years broke through

my skin. The days like dirt under my cabinets.

I age in a nation that imports its oranges.

At the grocery store, I weigh each fruit

against another. I inherited my grandmother's

shoulders. Heir to her sorrow, she named me *worthy*

of love and I don't know how to believe her.

At the self-checkout, I scan the barcode

on a solitary orange. Lonely in my apartment,

I break its brightness with my thumb.

YUZANA FOR THE MONSOON

Say you're older, and ever
the encroaching. Weather wrings
the only thing I own.

These cobblestones, these raindrops,
like caresses, stopped and sweet.
I raise my feet and wait.

The monsoon's fate: to shudder.
You spill out thunder, I sweep.
What can I keep? This rain—

emptying—stains rusting roofs.
And the proof is in the loss.
This is the cost: the hush,

shedding bottlebrush. The stone,
the water. The bones will bring
the sobering. Sever.

SALVAGE

Say I don't lose the diamond from his mother's ring.
Say I don't wait for the TikTok algorithm to tell me

Here's a message from someone who has passed.

Say the automated reader doesn't command

Forgive yourself for my death

and say I don't immediately think of my father.
Say I don't turn the house over, looking for a speck of star.

Say there's breath enough for both of us.
Say he spits and there's the diamond I didn't lose,

a pinprick, cold and lovely. Say the rain comes down
& my name is a prayer sticking to his lips.

Say I don't lose him to the thunder.
Say I'm not overhauling moth-dusted bed frames
for memories I swear I possess.

Say I'm a better daughter.

Look how tenderly I place a vase of water hyacinths
by his propped-up head. Look how I forgive him

for all the hurt purpling on my skin. Listen—
I'm singing his favorite song.

DECISIONS

My brother sends me out for tamarind water
& chickpea powder & fish sauce & onions & cilantro.
I'm making Burmese chicken salad.

My mother calls & comments about my eyeliner.
Make sure you take it off before you go to sleep.
Asks: *If I come to the States, could I stay with you?*

I treat it like an exercise: map out her arrival in O'Hare,
plan a bus ride to Madison. The couch can double
as a bed. I'll adjust to her breath in the next room.

& Surely I can feed her & surely she'd like it here.
On my way to the grocery store, I greet the ginkgoes—
trees I've befriended in this frozen place.

My mother tells me, *You'll catch a cold. Wear a hat.*
I send her a picture of the lake, riddled with snow.
She would learn to love it here. I'd get her health insurance.

Together we'll learn the names of her ailments, sprouting
like spring flowers: scoliosis. Varicose veins. Melancholia.
Inevitably, when the apartment becomes too small

for our bodies, we'll find something bigger. Somewhere
with a veranda. For her orchids. There are no monasteries
close to us so we'll set up a shrine. I'll buy effigies

of Buddhas on Etsy. She'll infuse them with prayer.

My brother will visit & the chicken salad will taste
sour-sweet on our changing tongues. When she misses home,

I'll teach her how to love a life still without its footing.
How to call ၛၟုၚ် by another name & chop it into a salad.
Even here, a similar surviving.

DEAR FELLOW FABLEMAKER,

There is a moral to this story,

although I am still figuring it out.

Last winter the lakes froze only

a little bit, and the tree that carries

the reddest cardinals is bare

of their feathers. I stepped out

once, on the ice. The fog came in.

The darkness was almost unbearable.

In the warmth, my brother and I

hung snowflakes on a Christmas tree.

I burned my wishes in a metal tray.

A man I fancied played *auld lang syne*

over the phone. I wondered: is this

mercy? When grief shines more kindly

through my suncatcher, red glass

shaped like a hummingbird. Splattered

light against the wall. This is a story

I'll tell someday, when they ask me

about the quiet. Believe: I've never

been safer. Here where the snow

raises the ground to meet me.

Here where the world ends,

and I don't end with it.

NOTES

Thank you to the editors of these publications where some of the poems in this collection first appeared, sometimes in a different form:

Baltimore Review: "Fable for a Father"
Beloit Poetry Journal: "Kin Ma" and "Cremating Our Fathers"
Black Warrior Review: "International Student"
Gavialidae: "Pagoda"
Grist Journal: "When I Am a Mother"
Guernica: "Histories"
HAD: "At Sixty, My Mother"
Honey Literary: "Burmese Pygmalion"
The Margins, AAWW: "On Being Absent for the Revolution"
POETRY: "Thoughts on Reincarnation"
Poetry Northwest: "Savage," "Out with Lanterns," and "I Was Always a Poet with a Dead Father"
Salt Hill Journal: "It's a Bad Year for the Ginkgoes"
West Trestle Review: "My Father Died"

The following poems have appeared in previously published chapbooks:

Monsoon Daughter, Thirty West Publishing House (2022): "Monsoon Daughter Tries Narrative Therapy," "At Sixty, My Mother," and "Yuzana for the Monsoon"

Unsprung, Newfound (2023): "Kin Ma," "On Being Absent for the Revolution," "Cremating Our Fathers," "When I Am a Mother," and "Yuzana for the Left Behind"

The epigraphs are from Maryhilda Obasiota Ibe's poem, "Aberration," Li-Young Lee's *The City in Which I Love You*, Sean Bishop's *The Night We're Not Sleeping In*, and Jean Valentine's *Shirt in Heaven*.

The italicized text in "Dear Fellow Fablemaker, [My country is governed by a constitution,]" is from the section titled "Provisions on a State of Emergency" from Myanmar's 2008 constitution. The poem owes its thanks to Hannah Keziah Agustin.

"Pagoda" owes its thanks to Kaveh Akbar, who offhandedly said during a craft talk, "A divine can be a country."

The yuzana is a nonce form, a meld of two Burmese poetical forms, the than-bauk and the ya-du. It comprises five stanzas, each a tercet, and utilizes a version of the climbing rhyme (it operates in a zigzag). The first two lines of each stanza are seven syllables, with the third having six. The rhymes in the final stanza reflect those in the first. The name *yuzana* is derived from its floral counterpart, a small, fragrant bloom with five petals.

ACKNOWLEDGMENTS

I am grateful for the support of the Creative Writing department at the University of Wisconsin–Madison and the Wisconsin Institute for Creative Writing, without which these poems would not exist.

Thank you to the entire team at Gaudy Boy and Singapore Unbound—Jee Leong Koh, Kimberley Lim, and Laetitia Keok, especially—for the care you've poured into shepherding *Fablemaker* into the world. I could not have asked for better stewards of my work. Thank you to Ng Yi-Sheng for selecting *Fablemaker* as the Gaudy Boy Poetry Book Prize winner. Thank you, Flora Chan, for the cover of my dreams.

Thank you to my teachers and mentors who encouraged me to pursue this strange ambition: Daw Yin Yin Thein, Daw Daisy Thida Aung, W. Hastings Hensel, Wyatt Prunty, Amy Quan Barry, Leila Chatti, and Erika Meitner. Thank you to everyone who's been in workshop with me, for seeing these poems in their earliest stages, for holding them with grace and care.

Thank you to Madison's own Poetry Book Club, for which I read Ama Codjoe's *Bluest Nude* and promptly decided to restructure my entire manuscript. On that note, thank you, Ama Codjoe, for writing such a stellar collection.

Thank you to my nearest and dearest fablemakers, with much love and ginkgo leaves: Meg Kim for *The Lord of the Rings* musical and Nando's chicken; Aurora Shimshak for crabapple rain and Madison Sourdough carrot cake; Renée Lepreau for ecstatic dance and Chihuahuan company (shoutout to Lou and Fran); Caleb Parker for beers at the Terrace and a lamp to write by; Nitya Gupta, Rob Sorrell Bynum, and Rachel Hawley for lake walks and momos at Little Tibet; Elijah Bean for the conversations—*can* soup be scrumptious?—; Sadia Hassan for drunken noodles and poems over the phone; Gothataone Moeng for Festy runs and international student solidarity; Ada Zhang for tea and Tofu sessions; Natasha Oladokun for poem insight and *Twilight* marathons; Gabriella Balza for goblin nights and atrocious accents; Sean Bishop for endless kindnesses and Oscar-worthy Hobbit Day performances; Ron Kuka for lakeside bonfires and *Wicked* excursions; Chessy Normile for acorn-shaped bloodstones and cabbage handoffs; Steven Espada Dawson for being the best poet laureate Madison, Wisconsin, could ask for; Winniebell Xinyu Zong for tiramisu and Global Market runs; Rodlyn-mae Banting for being an accomplice in yearning; Iqra Khan, Maryhilda Obasiota Ibe, Patrycja Humienik, juj e. lepe, Jonny Teklit, and Andrew Chi Keong Yim for poems that expand the breadth of my being; Kabel Mishka Ligot and Ajibola Tolase for lighting the way.

Khin Chan Myae Maung, for teaching me how to write toward Myanmar again; Dayana Ahamad, for her unwavering faith in me (love you, wing); Hannah Wood, for acts of care too numerous to count; Yousra Aisha Hussain, for the Good Times™; Sanika Shah, for a friendship that began in second grade and endures.

Al Bardi, still my first reader, for warmth and rants and almond cakes. Buck Butler, for so much patience and photos of the Guerry Garth ginkgo tree. Kristina Romanenkova, for dessert-making companionship and the love you bear my brother. My cat, Ginkgo Gaia Gourmet Bast, for finally adjusting to a reasonable feeding schedule.

My grandfathers, for the gift of meter and melody. My grandmothers, Winsome and Kitty, for haunting the narrative. Aunty Gyi, for loving me exactly how I am.

My father, for the fables, for the house with the yellow door, for a love as sharp, as soft, as a crocodile's maw. My mother, for the folktales, for the orchids that grace our veranda, for leaving when she did. My brother, for the green swing stories that saved us both, for goji berry tea, for making sure I am never lonely in this life.

And you, dear fellow fablemaker: thank you. Thank you for being a part of this story.

ABOUT THE AUTHOR

© Rob Sorrell Bynum

Mandy Moe Pwint Tu is a pile of ginkgo leaves in a trench coat from Yangon, Myanmar. Her work has appeared in POETRY, Beloit Poetry Journal, Porter House Review, Waxwing, and elsewhere. She has published three poetry chapbooks: *Monsoon Daughter* (Thirty West Publishing House, 2022), *Unsprung* (Newfound, 2023), and *Burma Girl* (Gold Line Press, 2026). She received her MFA from the University of Wisconsin–Madison, where she was the Hoffman-Halls Emerging Artist Fellow at the Wisconsin Institute for Creative Writing.

From the Latin *gaudium*, meaning "joy," Gaudy Boy publishes books that delight readers with the various powers of art. The name is taken from the poem "Gaudy Turnout," by Singaporean poet Arthur Yap, about his time abroad in Leeds, the United Kingdom. Similarly inspired by such diasporic wanderings and migrations, Gaudy Boy brings literary works by authors of Asian heritage to the attention of an American audience and beyond. Established in 2018 as the imprint of the New York City–based literary nonprofit Singapore Unbound, we publish poetry, fiction, and literary nonfiction.

Visit our website at www.singaporeunbound.org/gaudyboy.

Poetry

Fablemaker: Poems
by Mandy Moe Pwint Tu

Eke: Poems
by Wahidah Tambee

Interrogation Records: Poems
by Jeddie Sophronius

Waking Up to the Pattern Left by a Snail Overnight: Poems
by Jim Pascual Agustin

Time Regime: Poems
by Jhani Randhawa

Object Permanence: Poems
by Nica Bengzon

Play for Time: Poems
by Paula Mendoza

Autobiography of Horse: A Poem
by Jenifer Sang Eun Park

The Experiment of the Tropics: Poems
by Lawrence Lacambra Ypil

Fiction and Nonfiction

The Way You Want to Be Loved: Stories
by Aruni Kashyap

Lovelier, Lonelier: A Novel
by Daryl Qilin Yam

Bengal Hound: A Novel
by Rahad Abir

The Infinite Library and Other Stories
by Victor Fernando R. Ocampo

The Sweetest Fruits: A Novel
by Monique Truong

And the Walls Come Crumbling Down
by Tania De Rozario

The Foley Artist: Stories
by Ricco Villanueva Siasoco

Malay Sketches: Stories
by Alfian Sa'at

Other Series

New Singapore Poetries
edited by Marylyn Tan and Jee Leong Koh

Suspect: Volume 1, Year 1
edited by Jee Leong Koh

From Gaudy Boy Translates

Memorial Club: A Novel
by Mozid Mahmud

Picking off new shoots will not stop the spring:
Witness Poems and Essays from Burma/Myanmar 1988–2021
edited by Ko Ko Thett and Brian Haman

Amanat: Women's Writing from Kazakhstan
edited by Zaure Batayeva and Shelley Fairweather-Vega

Ulirát: Best Contemporary Stories in Translation from the Philippines
edited by Tilde Acuña, John Bengan, Daryll Delgado, Amado Anthony G.
Mendoza III, and Kristine Ong Muslim

Books by our other imprint, Bench Press

Sample and Loop: A Simple History of Singaporeans in America
by Jee Leong Koh

Snow at 5 PM: Translations of an Insignificant Japanese Poet
by Jee Leong Koh

Seven Studies for a Self-Portrait: Poems
by Jee Leong Koh

Equal to the Earth: Poems
by Jee Leong Koh

Lightly in the Good of Day: Poems
by Bob Hart

Try to Have Your Writing Make Sense:
The Quintessential PFFA Anthology: Poems
edited by Donna Smith and Howard Miller

www.ingramcontent.com/pod-product-compliance
Lightning Source LLC
Chambersburg PA
CBHW031433120626
46545CB00006B/2383

* 9 781958 652183 *